I Wonder Why

Whales Sing

and Other Questions About Sea Life

Caroline Harris

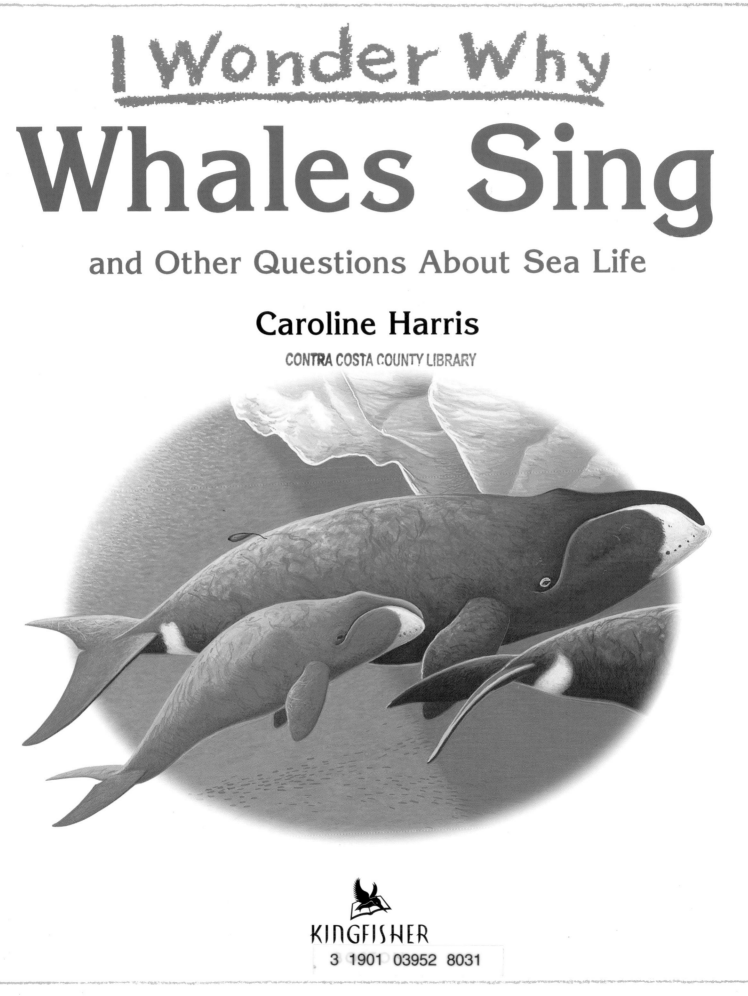

KINGFISHER

KINGFISHER

a Houghton Mifflin Company
 imprint
222 Berkeley Street
Boston, Massachusetts 02116
www.houghtonmifflinbooks.com

First published in 2006
10 9 8 7 6 5 4 3 2 1

1TR/0106/SHE/RNB(RNB)/126.6MA/F

LIBRARY OF CONGRESS CATALOGING-IN-PUBLICATION DATA
has been applied for.

ISBN 0-7534-5965-5
ISBN 978-07534-5965-2

Senior editor: Belinda Weber
Coordinating editor: Caitlin Doyle
Art editor and visualizer: Dominic Zwemmer
DTP manager: Nicky Studdart
DTP operator: Claire Cessford
Artwork archivist: Wendy Allison
Production controller: Lindsey Scott
Proofreader and indexer: Sheila Clewley
Illustrations:
Martin Camm 4–5, 8–9, 10–11, 14–15,
        16–17, 20–21, 22–23, 26–27, 30–31;
Michael Langham Rowe 6–7, 12–13, 18–19,
        24–25, 28–29;
Peter Wilks (SGA) all cartoons.

Printed in Taiwan

CONTENTS

4 Why don't fish drown?

5 Why do divers need headlights?

5 Where does grass grow underwater?

6 Which animal swims by waving?

6 Why are octopuses like jet planes?

7 Why does a fish need fins?

8 Which fish uses a rod to catch its food?

8 Which creature uses combs to eat?

9 What looks like a flower but really is a trap?

10 Which crab borrows its house?

10 Which shellfish digs with its foot?

11 Why do some fish have eyes on their sides?

12 Why are lionfish like porcupines?

12 Which fish wears armor?

13 What hides in ink?

14 Why do baby dolphins need guards?

15 What jumps up waterfalls?

15 What is busy during a full moon?

16 Where can you see smoke?

17 What are sponges?

17 Which animals march in a line?

18 Which part of the ocean is the brainiest?

19 What lettuce would make a nasty sandwich?

19 What has a funny home?

20 Why do whales sing?

20 What is spyhopping?

21 What causes strandings?

22 How do dolphins stand up?

22 What is like an elephant?

23 How do seals and sea lions stay warm?

24 How do sharks find their food?

24 What is strange about a shark's skeleton?

25 What use is a long tail?

25 How dangerous are sharks?

26 Which fish has binoculars?

27 What looks like the night sky?

27 When is a spider not a spider?

28 Which bird hangs its wings to dry?

28 Why do crabs run sideways?

29 Which lizard goes swimming?

30 What is whale watching?

31 How can satellites help sea creatures?

31 Who cleans beaches?

Why don't fish drown?

Humans can't breathe in water, but fish can. Oxygen is found in water and in air. In order to breathe, fish gulp in water. Instead of lungs, they have red, frilly flaps called gills on each side of their head.

Gill slit

● When water flows over a fish's gills, the oxygen in it passes into the fish's blood. Long, curved slits let the water out.

● A glass of seawater is full of minerals called salts and millions of tiny plants and animals known as plankton.

Mouth

Gills

● At 98 feet (30m) long and weighing up to 190 tons, the blue whale is the biggest animal on Earth. It's as long as 18 adults swimming in a line, head to toe. But its favorite food, a shrimplike animal called krill, is tiny. It is only an inch or two long!

● All land animals descended from sea creatures. Millions of years ago the first animals crept out of the water to start life on land.

Why do divers need headlights?

Only the first 656 feet (200m) below the surface of the ocean are lit by the sun. This is where all sea plants and most sea creatures live. Below that is the murky twilight zone. The midnight zone, from 3,280 feet (1,000m) down, is completely dark.

Angelfish

Sunlight zone

656 feet (200m)

Twilight zone

Midnight zone

Abyssal zone

Dugong

Sea grass

Where does grass grow underwater?

Sea grass grows in shallow water and is the only ocean plant that has flowers. In warm waters dugongs graze on it. Dugongs are also known as sea cows.

● Life on Earth began in the seas more than 3.5 billion years ago. People have found fossils of these ancient animals.

Which animal swims by waving?

Rays have wide, strong side fins that make them look like underwater kites. The ray's muscles make these fins move in a wave. The ripple begins at the front, where the fins connect to the head, and travels to the back, pushing the ray through the water. Rays are flat, and they often glide along close to the seabed— but their closest cousins are sharks!

Octopus moving through the water

• The by-the-wind sailor jellyfish has a flat "sail" that it holds at an angle to the wind. It is blown across the ocean surface, like a sailboat.

Why are octopuses like jet planes?

Octopuses, squid, cuttlefish, and scallops all use jet propulsion to speed through the sea. Octopuses pump water in over their gills and squirt it out through a fleshy tube called a siphon. They can point the siphon in almost any direction, which helps them steer.

● Starfish crawl along on thousands of tube feet. Each one has to reach forward in the direction that the starfish wants to move.

Manta ray

● Turtles are reptiles, but instead of four legs, they have flat flippers. A turtle beats its front pair of flippers like wings to "fly" through the water.

● Some types of fish can "walk." Batfish have a pair of long, thick fins underneath their body. They use these to creep along the seabed.

Why does a fish need fins?

Fish use their fins to move them along, as well as for balance, steering, braking, and swimming backward. Fish wriggle through the water, similar to a snake, but they also swish their tail fins for extra speed. Other fins help them stay level.

Which fish uses a rod to catch its food?

The anglerfish has a long spine on its head with a lure on the end that it shakes to attract smaller fish—like someone with a fishing rod. The lures of deep-sea anglerfish even glow so that they can catch fish in the dark.

● Electric rays and stargazer fish are among the 250 types of creatures that can give the animals they hunt a bad electric shock. They have special organs that work like batteries.

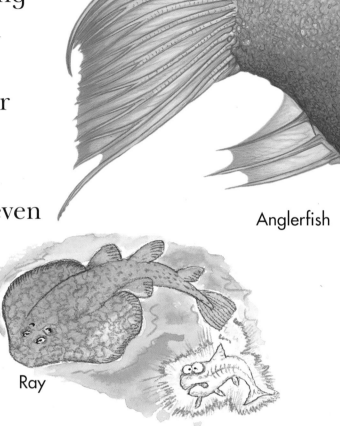

Anglerfish

Ray

Which creature uses combs to eat?

Many of the largest whales are filter feeders and eat by pushing water through rows of tightly packed plates in their mouths. Plankton and small fish get caught in these combs, called

Right whale

baleen, and can be swallowed.

Lure

- Tiny cleaner fish dart into the mouths of sharks and other fish to feed on scraps of food that are caught in their teeth. Luckily for the cleaner fish, the sharks don't eat their living toothbrushes!

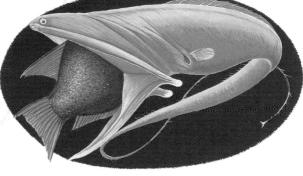

- The jaws of a gulper eel open so wide it can swallow a fish that is much larger than itself. It needs to grab any fish that pass by, since food is hard to find deep in the sea.

What looks like a flower but really is a trap?

Sea anemones are named after a flower because their tentacles open up like petals during high tide. But shrimps or small fish that brush past these "flowers" get a terrible sting. This stuns the fish so that the sea anemone can eat them.

Which crab borrows its house?

Most crabs are protected by a hard casing all over their bodies, but the hermit crab is not as tough. Its shell is very thin, so it needs something tougher to make a safe home. It finds an empty shell, backs into it, and walks away with a new house.

Which shellfish digs with its foot?

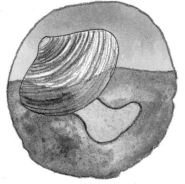

Many types of clams burrow into the seabed and then stay there. They have a strong "foot" made out of muscle that anchors them into the sand. A clam's shell has two halves, which it can close tightly if it is threatened.

• Cuttlefish can trick any animals that want to eat them by changing their color and pattern. They do this to match the part of the seabed they are swimming over.

Flounder

Why do some fish have eyes on their sides?

Flatfish, such as plaice, sole, and flounder, lie on their sides on the seabed to hide from enemies. The "side" that is on top changes color to match the ocean floor. One eye also moves around to this side so that it won't be buried in the mud.

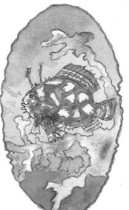

• Sargassum fish look like seaweed, but don't be fooled! These fish aren't shy and retiring— they are fierce fighters.

• Tower shells and mussels are mollusks. These creatures have soft bodies, but they can build hard shells around themselves.

Tower shell

Mussels

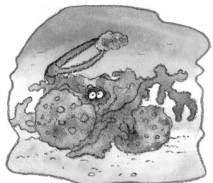

• Decorator crabs drape seaweed and sponges over their shells. It might not be the height of fashion, but it helps them hide from enemies.

Why are lionfish like porcupines?

From a distance a lionfish looks like it has a mane. But get up close, and you'll find that this fish's spikes are deadlier than its bite. When an enemy is nearby, the lionfish spreads out its fins, showing off its long spines. Anything that swims too close to it risks getting speared!

● The Australian box jellyfish, or sea wasp, is more dangerous than a cobra. Its venom can kill a person in a few minutes.

Which fish wears armor?

With many hungry sea animals ready to devour them, smaller creatures need to carry protection. Instead of ordinary scales, the boxfish is covered with six-sided, bony plates that are fused together to make stiff armor. Only its mouth, eyes, and fins can move freely.

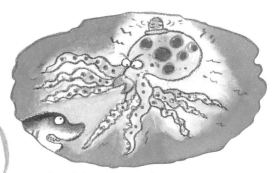

● The blue-ringed octopus gives a warning about its deadly bite. Usually it is brown, but when it is angry, it turns bright yellow with vivid blue circles.

● Some types of cone snails have a kind of long "nose" that looks like a tasty worm. When a fish tries to bite it, the snail shoots out a poisoned spike into its mouth.

What hides in ink?

Squid and their relatives shoot out a dark liquid, known as ink, to help them make a quick getaway. They squirt the ink from a tube that is close to their head, clouding the water and making it difficult for an enemy to see. The squid can then jet away.

Why do baby dolphins need guards?

A young dolphin, called a calf, needs to be protected from sharks and other enemies at all times. If the mother has to leave her calf to find food, other females guard the baby from enemies.

● Blue mussels produce an incredible twelve million eggs at a time. A lot won't survive, but with so many eggs, thousands will still hatch.

● Killer whales, or orcas, can live in their family group, known as a pod, for their entire lives. Despite their name, killer whales are actually large dolphins and do not harm humans.

● Jawfish fathers take parenting seriously. They store the female's eggs in their mouths to keep them safe until the eggs hatch. When the male eats, he puts the eggs in his burrow.

What jumps up waterfalls?

Atlantic salmon spend most of their lives at sea, but they swim back to the river where they were born when it's time to breed. They battle against the flow of the river, and some even have to leap up waterfalls.

● Male cod do an elaborate twisting and turning dance to impress their chosen partner.

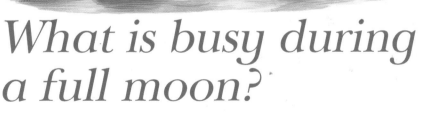

What is busy during a full moon?

During full moons in the spring thousands of horseshoe crabs travel along Pacific beaches and the east coast of the U.S. to lay their eggs. During the next full moon the baby horseshoe crabs hatch and return to the sea.

Where can you see smoke?

Cracks in the deep ocean floor spew out water that has been heated up in Earth's crust. The water can reach 842°F (450°C)—twice as hot as most ovens. It contains particles from the rocks that it has passed through, which appear as billowing clouds of smoke.

● Piddocks burrow into rocks by twisting around so that their rough front end drills into the rock. They never leave their caves once they have made them.

● Sea pens, which are related to jellyfish, look like old-fashioned quill pens. Add some squid ink, and you could write an underwater letter!

What are sponges?

Most bath sponges are now made out of plastic, but natural sponges are the skeletons of living sea creatures. Sponges are very simple creatures. They collect tiny particles of food by pumping water through their bodies.

● Sea mice have yellow fur and live in burrows. But they aren't mice at all—they're worms. They live in shallow water and push themselves through the sand and mud.

Which animals march in a line?

Spiny lobsters walk in a row along the ocean floor on their five pairs of legs. The line can be up to 60 lobsters long, and they sometimes travel nine miles (15km) per day. Each one keeps in touch with the lobster in front of it by using its feelers, or antennae.

Which part of the ocean is the brainiest?

Coral reefs are the home of corals of all shapes and sizes. They are made up of millions of animals called polyps that build stony skeletons. When the polyps die, the skeletons are left behind, and the living coral makes a new layer on top.

Sea fan

Brain coral

Staghorn coral

• Sometimes an entire coral reef will release billions of eggs at the same time, making a snowstorm in the ocean.

• Brightly colored moray eels hide inside of dark cracks in the coral. They lie in wait and then strike passing fish, grabbing them with their razor-sharp teeth.

What lettuce would make a nasty sandwich?

A lettuce slug might look like a crunchy leaf, but this is a disguise to trick its enemies. The sea slugs that live on coral reefs are as colorful as the fish. This is often a warning that they taste bad or are poisonous to eat.

Tubular sponge

● Coral reefs face many dangers. Some fishermen use dynamite to kill fish, and this damages the reefs. They are also eaten by crown of thorns starfish.

What has a funny home?

The clown fish is one of the many bright fish that lives in coral reefs. It lives in the stinging tentacles of a sea anemone, but it isn't hurt because its skin is covered with slimy mucus that protects it. The clown fish is safe from attacks, and the sea anemone can feast on its leftover catch.

Humpback whale

Why do whales sing?

Whales are talkative animals. They bellow, grunt, yelp, and make bubbling noises to find other whales and send messages. Male humpback whales sing long tunes, sometimes repeating them for hours or days. This is probably to attract a mate.

● The sperm whale is an incredible diver. It can hold its breath for more than two hours and can dive more than one mile (2km).

What is spyhopping?

Because whales and dolphins are mammals—like humans—they have to breathe air, so they are often seen at the surface. Spyhopping is when they stick their heads straight out of the water, often to look for food such as seals resting on the ice.

● If a whale is injured, others in the same group gather around to protect it.

● A baby blue whale weighs four tons at birth—the same as an adult hippopotamus or a medium-sized truck—and is 26 feet (8m) long. The next biggest baby is the fin whale, which weighs two tons.

What causes strandings?

Occasionally whales get stranded on beaches. No one knows why they do it, but people can help save their lives by keeping them damp and making sure that their blowholes are clear of sand and water so that they can breathe.

How do dolphins stand up?

A dolphin's tail is very powerful. It is so strong that dolphins can leap straight out of the sea and stand up. The tail moves up and down, not side to side, like a fish. The sweep of the tail pushes the dolphin through the water.

What is like an elephant?

Walrus have leathery skin and tusks, similar to elephants, that can be almost three feet (1m) long. These tusks are very large upper teeth that grow throughout their lives.

● At 16 feet long (5m) male elephant seals are the giants of the seal world. They spend most of their lives out at sea and only come to shore to find a mate.

● From a distance—and in the moonlight, when they like to feed—manatees and dugongs can look strangely human. In the past they have been mistaken for mermaids!

How do seals and sea lions stay warm?

Many sea mammals have a thick layer of fat called blubber beneath their skin to hold the heat in. Some seals and sea lions have hair, and others have thick, furry coats with a second layer of shorter hair close to the skin to keep the water out.

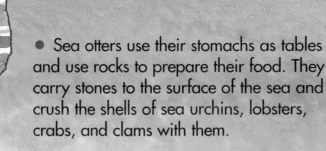

● Sea otters use their stomachs as tables and use rocks to prepare their food. They carry stones to the surface of the sea and crush the shells of sea urchins, lobsters, crabs, and clams with them.

How do sharks find their food?

Sharks use six senses to find their next meal. They can see better than humans can and can sniff out blood in the water that is hundreds of feet away. They can also sense the small amounts of electricity that are given off by all living things.

● Sharks aren't fussy eaters. They swallow whatever they can find in the sea, including tin cans, leather jackets— and even a bottle of wine!

What is strange about a shark's skeleton?

The skeletons of most fish are bony, but a shark's skeleton is made of cartilage. This is the springy material that gives your nose and ears their shape. Sharkskin is covered in toothlike scales that make it as rough as sandpaper.

What use is a long tail?

The thresher shark's tail is almost as long as its body. The shark whips its tail from side to side to herd fish into a group. The force of the lashes also stuns the fish so that the thresher shark can snap them up with its strong teeth.

● The nurse shark grows a new set of teeth every week. Other sharks have extra rows of teeth in case some of them wear out.

How dangerous are sharks?

Most species of sharks aren't dangerous to humans and only eat tiny plankton and fish. Some shark attacks against people might be a case of mistaken identity. Surfers can look like seals from underneath the water, and some sharks snack on these sea mammals.

Which fish has binoculars?

Some unusual creatures live deep in the ocean. The gigantura has tube-shaped eyes with bulging lenses that look like binoculars. These help it see even the faintest glow from its prey. Hatchetfish have strange eyes that can only look upward.

Hatchetfish

Gigantura

Viperfish

Black dragon

● At 16,400 feet (5,000m) the pressure of the water is so strong that it would crush your body. But animals have to live, swim, and eat there!

● No one has ever seen a full grown adult colossal squid, but scientists believe that it would be almost 60 feet (18m).

● The tripod fish spends most of its life standing around. It perches on three thin fins and waits for its dinner to bump into it.

Anglerfish

Lantern fish

What looks like the night sky?

Lantern fish are spotted with small, shiny dots, so they look like clusters of stars as they swim along. But they're not alone—most deep-sea animals can make their own light. This helps them recognize each other in the dark!

● Red opossum shrimps shoot out liquid that bursts into clouds of light. This confuses any fish that try to eat them.

When is a spider not a spider?

Sea spiders are cousins of land spiders, but they are a separate type called pycnogonids. Sea spiders don't scurry—they creep along on their spindly legs so that they don't stir up the slimy goo on the seabed.

Which bird hangs its wings to dry?

Cormorants dive into the ocean to catch eels and fish, then come ashore and perch on a rock, holding out their wings. Their feathers do not have the waterproofing oils that cover most other seabirds, so they need to be dried out by the sun and breeze.

● Eiders are sea ducks that live on rocky coasts and enjoy eating crabs. Quilts used to be filled with their fluffy feathers.

● Most starfish have either five arms or a multiple of five such as ten or 20. If one of the arms breaks off, the starfish grows another one!

Why do crabs run sideways?

Crabs have their skeletons on the outside as a hard shell that covers their bodies. Most crabs can walk any way they want, but the leg joints of some crabs only move in one direction, like your knee or your elbow. This makes it easiest to scurry.

- Emperor penguins balance their eggs on their feet and protect them from the Antarctic chill with a built-in "egg warmer."

Which lizard goes swimming?

The marine iguana, found on the Galápagos Islands, is the only sea lizard. It swims underwater to eat seaweed, but it has to quickly do some sunbathing after a dip in the cold sea. It is cold-blooded and needs the sun to warm it up.

- Cowrie shells have been used as money in more places around the world than any coin! In the past you could buy and sell with them in countries from India to the U.S.

- The frigate bird, which soars over tropical seas, has a bright red neck pouch that it blows up like a balloon. It does this to show off to females.

What is whale watching?

Many tourists now go out on boat trips to watch whales in their natural surroundings. Whale watching helps people understand more about these special creatures and makes sure that the places where they live are kept safe.

● Throughout history sailors have told tales of terrifying sea monsters. But we now know that most of these monsters are just ordinary sea creatures.

● Some fishing boats drag huge nets through the water, catching lots of fish. But this has made some fish very rare and may even damage the seabed.

How can satellites help sea creatures?

Special tags that have been attached to bowhead whales and other sea animals send signals to satellites out in space. This allows scientists to track where the whales go and helps us learn more about them. We can then protect them better.

- Purple dye, which was made by crushing lots of tiny sea snails, was used to color the robes of ancient kings.

- In Japan puffer fish is an expensive treat—but if you eat the wrong parts, the fish's poison will kill you!

Who cleans beaches?

Sometimes sticky oil spills out of ships that carry it, polluting the sea and beaches. It poisons sea creatures and can even kill them. Teams of people clean up the beaches to save the animals' lives.

Index

A

anglerfish 8
Atlantic salmon 15

B

baleen 8
batfish 7
blubber 23
boxfish 12

C

cartilage 24
clams 10
cleaner fish 9
clown fish 19
cone snails 13
coral reefs 18
cormorants 28
cowrie shells 29
crabs 10, 11, 15, 23, 28
cuttlefish 6, 11

D

dolphins 14, 15, 22, 23
dugongs 5, 23

E

eels 18, 28
eggs 14, 15, 18, 29
eiders 28
electric rays 8
elephant seals 22
emperor penguins 29

F

fins 6, 7, 12, 26
flatfish 11
frigate birds 29

G

giganturas 26
gills 4, 6
gulper eels 9

H

hatchetfish 26

J

jawfish 14
jellyfish 6, 12, 16

K

killer whales 14
krill 4

L

lantern fish 27
lettuce slugs 19
lionfish 12, 13

M

manatees 23
marine iguanas 29
mussels 14

O

octopuses 6, 13
oil spills 31
orcas see
    killer whales

P

piddocks 16
plankton 4, 8, 25
polyps 18
puffer fish 31

R

rays 6, 8

S

sargassum fish 11
satellites 31
scientists 4, 26, 31
sea anemones 9, 19
sea cows see dugongs
sea grass 5
sea mice 17
sea otters 23
sea pens 16
sea spiders 27
sea urchins 23
sea lions 23
seals 20, 22,
    23, 25
seaweed 11, 29
sharks 6, 9, 24, 25
shellfish 10
shells 10, 11, 29
shrimps 4, 9, 27
skeletons 17, 18, 24, 28
spiny lobsters 17
sponges 11, 17
spyhopping 20
squid 6, 13, 16, 26
starfish 7, 19
stargazer fish 8
strandings 21

T

teeth 9, 18, 22, 25
tentacles 9
tower shells 11
tripod fish 26
turtles 7

W

walrus 22
whales 4, 8, 14,
    20–21, 30–31
whale watching 30